Karma

A GUIDE TO
CAUSE AND EFFECT

DEDICATION

This book is dedicated to the many
great teachers of the Hindu/Vedic
Sanatana Dharma knowledge. Their
wisdom and personal examples of
holy living have guided my efforts
in creating this small contribution
to understanding who we are and
our greater purpose for being here.

MANDALA
WISDOM
SERIES

Karma

A GUIDE TO
CAUSE AND EFFECT

JEFFREY ARMSTRONG
(KAVINDRA RISHI)

MANDALA
San Rafael, California

TABLE OF

CONTENTS

INTRODUCTION

When you speak badly of others,
you eat their karma.

Of all the subjects that are crucial to us human beings, *karma*—or ultimate cause and effect—is one of the most important. Karma is about all of the things we do and the results that proceed from that doing. Karma is a Sanskrit word that comes to us from the Vedas, the library of spiritual books from India. Sanskrit is a very precise language, used throughout ancient history as a scientific language to record the results of human experience in both material and spiritual matters. Modern linguists recognize that Aramaic, Greek, Latin romance languages, and English are largely rooted in Sanskrit origins. Karma is an ancient concept, with at least a ten-thousand-year cultural history in India. Before there was modern science with its notion that "every action has an equal and opposite reaction," ancient thinkers throughout the East studied karma as the science of the reactions to everything we do.

The word karma stems from the Sanskrit root *kri*, which means "to do." The English word *create* is derived from this root. The idea is that everything that surrounds us is interconnected in causal chains that are not always obvious. And as we engage in actions, we desire the ability to predict their outcomes. It is for this reason that modern science has based its progress upon repeatable experiments. Repeatable means that there is a predictable outcome to certain specific actions. In a limited sense, this is also karma, the science of understanding how the outcome is related to our behavior—to what we do.

The scientific thinkers of ancient India also studied material nature in exactly that way, in terms of cause and effect. But they realized that in order to ultimately understand what we do and our actions' long-term implications, we also have to understand three other things. One of those is the individual doer, the second is material nature, and the third is the Supreme Controller or Divine Intelligence. In other words, cause and effect are not just about the mechanical operations of matter; they are also about who we are in essence and what our ultimate destination could be, as well as our relationship with the Supreme Being and the various laws of nature. Karma raises the questions of who we are in the final state of our being, where we come from, why we are here, who or what is in control of the universe, and what possibilities are there beyond our present experiences. Karma not only asks how we can interact with and control the world around us,

but also brings forward the moral questions of what right and wrong actions are and what the future consequences of our present actions will be. How long do we, and the cause and effect resulting from our actions, continue into the future?

It is for this reason that we often hear the words *karma* and *reincarnation* in the same sentence. The missing question regarding cause and effect that modern science and many religions have failed to consider is this: What if we, the doers, are neither the body nor the mind? What if we are indestructible conscious entities that move from body to body, life after life, creating and receiving the results of our various doings? It is very likely that one of the reasons science has avoided these questions is because of their problematic history with the medieval Catholic Church. Since independent scientific thinking was persecuted and often punishable by death at the hands of religion, it is natural that the scientists of that era were apprehensive of the danger and subsequently divorced themselves from spiritual questions of life that could challenge the ruling religious elite. But in India, no such persecution of scientific thinking ever occurred. There, the widely accepted rule was tolerance of various philosophies and worldviews. Thus it was only natural for the Indian approach to karma to include materialistic, existential, scientific, philosophical, and spiritual components.

The main question that lies at the root of India's spiritual schools of thought is this: Who or what is the Ultimate Source of the laws of nature? These laws imply both purpose and intelligence, including a lawmaker and finally a long-term view of the soul and its relation to cause and effect as an evolutionary process over many lifetimes. From the Indian perspective, any science is incomplete unless it addresses ultimate questions as well as temporal ones. This, at least, is the view promoted by the Vedic library of knowledge that first gave rise to the study of karma as a science. Unlike many religions or traditions that limit their source of information to one or a very few books, the culture of India has a large library of books on hundreds of material and spiritual subjects. Those texts are called the Vedas and are all written in the ancient and scientific Sanskrit language. That body of knowledge has been carefully preserved and handed down over the last ten thousand years. The information on karma in this book has been extracted and summarized from those Vedic sources. Of course, discussions on some of the principles of karmic science are present in most philosophies and traditions. You will no doubt see similarities and differences with the Vedic view as you study the subject more deeply.

Once we include the bigger questions of nature, our own eternal nature, and the intention of the Supreme Being into the question of cause and effect, karma becomes a pivotal part of a much larger conversation. If, as the Vedas suggest, we really are eternal beings, then the things that we do by using our free will have the potential to unfold over very long periods of time, with very complex consequences. If we extend the boundary of our thinking beyond the limits of just one lifetime, then our continual reincarnation appears to be directed by the cause and effect that result from our personal choices and actions. In that case, cause and effect need to be studied over many lifetimes, and justice, or the balancing of the scales of action and reaction, will be played out over a much longer period of time. Such a view will also include a system of administration of cause and effect, some method by which the delivery of so many causal chains is interwoven and connected.

This is the rationale behind the ancient science of *Jyotisha*, or Vedic astrology, which is very different from the astrology as entertainment we often see today. According to Vedic astrology, if we are souls investing our free will through actions, then a trail of reactions is always following along behind us as the delayed result of our actions. It also follows that somewhere in us and the universe, there must be a record-keeping department concerned with the balancing of the cosmic books. Someone and something must be monitoring the delivery of the results of the actions of all these humans who are using free will to invest in certain kinds of work. The theory behind astrology then is that encoded in the positions of the planets and stars at the location and moment of birth is information about the nature and delivery schedule of the past actions carried by each soul. The delivery

of that cause and effect is carried out by divine helpers working on behalf of the Supreme Being.

This means that some but not all of our life is predetermined by our previous use of free will. It means that the Divine Intelligence of the universe has a longer memory than us and that "what goes around comes around" may be on a longer trajectory than we have so far imagined. The greatness of karma as a philosophical concept and practical understanding is that it sees a soul's journey of evolution on a very grand scale. It is a view that envisions the continual evolution of countless trillions of souls over vast stretches of space and tremendous eras of cosmic time. You could say that karma is the judicial system of a great intergalactic federation of democratic action run by free will in a context of Divine law.

Seen from this perspective, each time we take on a body or are born again as a human, we are both receiving old karma and creating new karma. Finally, this also raises the questions of whether or not, and how, we might escape the limitations and suffering of this cycle of cause and effect and be restored to our original nature, which the Vedas depict as an eternal joyful soul in a transcendental world. Since cause and effect appear to us as a cycle, they may be viewed as a circle. We initiate an action and at a certain time in the future, we reap the fruit of our deeds. It resembles the agricultural cycle in the circle of the year. We sow seeds and then garner the rewards—"As you sow, so you shall reap." Karma is the science of our actions and their outcomes.

The larger process of the soul transmigrating from life to life and body to body over many lifetimes is called *samsara* in Sanskrit; it is the wheel of repeated birth and death from life to life. The concept of karma then includes both the short-term cause and effect cycle—the moral consequences implied in "do unto others as you would have them do unto you"—and the long-term evolution of all the souls over many lifetimes. As we will see, the implications of this view form a grand and profound cosmology that is the basis of what we have come to think of as the "Eastern" view, a view deeply influenced by Vedic thought. Now, due to the effects of technology, East and West have not only met but are increasingly part of one world that we are changing very rapidly by all we do. Our current level of ability to alter the balance of natural law calls into question everything we do. At present we are gambling with our children's futures and perhaps the future of life on our planet. Never has there been a time when an understanding of karma was more relevant than it is today.

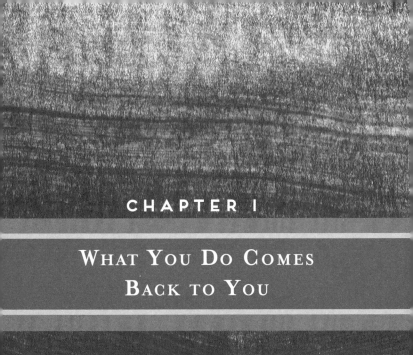

CHAPTER 1

WHAT YOU DO COMES BACK TO YOU

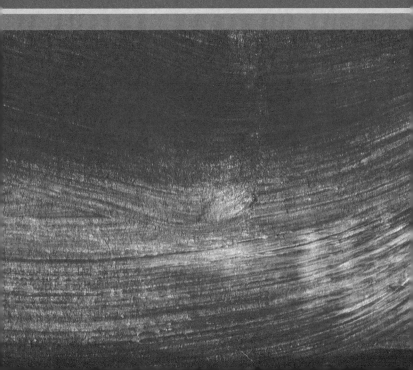

What You Do

Comes Back to You

Cause is effect concealed,
effect is cause revealed.

The Vedic concept of karma is based upon the existence of three eternal realities. The first is a transcendental or nonmaterial realm that is not currently visible to us. That place is described in the Vedas as existing eternally without the need for Sun, Moon, or electricity. It is self-luminous, completely conscious, and full of all the beauty we experience here but without the presence of birth, death, old age, or disease. Naturally, from where we stand at the moment, we are inclined to doubt the existence of this other realm, since we do not have direct experience of it. But the Vedic literature is very explicit and detailed in its descriptions of that transcendental abode.

THE UNCONSCIOUS REALM ❧

The second eternal reality is the material world where we currently reside. It is called *prakriti* or *maya*, the dark unconscious energy, and is real but temporary. Everything here within matter is transitory; it is created, exists for a while, and is then destroyed. Unlike the transcendental abode, which is made of a conscious energy, the material world is made of an unconscious energy. In this world, everything is subject to birth, death, old age, and disease or dissolution. The world we view through our senses is fraught with limitation. The beauty we experience, although real, is mixed up with the temporary qualities of matter. In simple terms, this is the cause of our frustration with life. Life is a struggle to get the things we want within matter, and then there is a struggle to keep them, often leading to conflict or war. Eventually we all lose that struggle at the final moment of the death of our bodies. Therefore, the material world is known as the place where everything dies. In spite of this transitory nature, matter itself is also described as an eternally existing reality, though it is temporary in the sense that the soul can be freed from it.

MANY ETERNAL SOULS ❧

The third eternal reality is us, the many eternal souls, some of whom have come to visit the material world. According to the Vedas, many more like us have remained in the transcendental world. The name for these countless individual souls is *atma*. The atmas are eternal, conscious, joyful, and individual in nature, but each soul eternally has the choice to reside in either the transcendental or material realms. If we choose to explore matter, as we have, then the natural result is that we go on a long journey exploring the material world.

In the process, we forget our transcendental origin. The atmas who come to the material realm are then called *jiva-atmas*, since they are in touch with material life (the words "viva" and "live" come from the Sanskrit *jiva*). Since by nature we are eternal, conscious, joyful, and unique, our visit to matter does not remove our original nature—it merely covers it over with layers of the dark and unconscious matter.

Unlike some traditions, the Vedas do not say that the souls coming into matter are bad or evil for doing so. Coming here is a part of our education as souls, and we each personally chose to come on this material adventure. If you like, think of the material world as a grand amusement park. A long time ago, we lived in the eternal realm. Then, at a certain point, we chose to enter the park, slid down a great long tunnel, and began the slow and very interesting exploration of the realm of matter. Once inside, all souls need an appropriate suit to function within the park's atmosphere. This suit is the material body. Think of it as a kind of diving suit made of matter. In Sanskrit, that matter is also called *gu*, which is humorously close to the English word goo. We come to the park as eternal souls and go from one body of goo to another, temporarily forgetful of our origin and true nature. Once in the goo or *prakriti*, we are convinced that our material body is our self. This is necessary in order for us to feel we are the enjoyer, which is the reason why we entered the park in the first place. We identify self with matter from that point onward until we learn otherwise. As we will see, that step of radical evolution is only possible once we reach human life.

8.4 MILLION SPECIES OF LIFE ❧

According to the Vedic scriptures, there are 8.4 million different species of life throughout the material realm. Of these, 8 million are subhuman, while 4 hundred thousand are varieties of human beings. The word *atma* is the origin of the English word *atomic*. Once the atomic particle of eternal consciousness enters into matter, it starts at the bottom of the evolutionary hierarchy and takes on a body. In that sense the Vedas would agree with Darwin that we do indeed evolve, but the Vedas say our evolution is not from matter, but rather within matter, an evolution of consciousness. Our eternal

soul climbs up the staircase of life, experiencing every species as a kind of learning by being and doing. From the smallest microbe up to insects, plants, birds, and mammals, we ascend the ladder of the species until we finally reach the lowest rung of human consciousness.

THE AMUSEMENT PARK IN THE SKY ✻

Try to picture the whole process as a walk through an immense cyber–amusement park, where you put on a different body to go on each ride. For the soul it is the same. It is just like the way we change clothes yet remain the same person. The Vedas describe the universe as a grand school for gradual evolution of our consciousness, a "universe-ity" where all the atmas are in different grades (bodies) learning all the lessons (or going on all the rides) in the beautiful material park. Of course, in between each new birth, the last body must die. This process is called *samsara* in Sanskrit, or the wheel of birth and death. Think of it as a kind of merry-go-round or Ferris wheel, in the amusement park of material life. This wheel of repeated birth and death promises pleasures; it delivers some but with them come many pains, disappointments, and sufferings of all descriptions.

THE DIFFERENCE BETWEEN HUMANS AND ANIMALS ✻

You have probably noticed that one of the differences between animals and humans is the amount of free will or choice that they can exercise. Animals and the beings below them are not able to exercise free will and self-awareness at the same level as humans. It is interesting to note that the word *mankind* comes from a Sanskrit word *manusha*. It does not mean "male," as you might think. It comes from the word *manas*, meaning "mind." In this context, it refers to humans as "having a mind of their own." Humans have reflective and moral minds that can distinguish between good and bad. The difference between the reflective minds of humans and the instinctual minds of animals and the species below them is that the instinctive mind does not generate karma through its actions. It lives and dies in a life of instinctual experience with no future consequences. But at the human stage, as we begin to reawaken to our true nature, we enter into the karma-generating stage of the evolutionary process. Once we are human, it is our actions and not our instincts that direct our evolutionary progress.

OLD SOULS AND YOUNG SOULS �

Newly arriving humans are not always certain whether they are animals or humans or some mixture of both. They have just spent many lifetimes in the various animal species, so it takes some time for the human qualities to become stronger than the animal characteristics. There are four activities that humans share with animals: eating, sleeping, mating, and defending. If those four activities occupy most of our mental energy, we are more animal than human in temperament. When our human side emerges it is accompanied by questions about who we are, such as: Why was I born? Why do I get sick? Why do I age? Why must I die? If you think again of the amusement park, the question for us is: What do we want to experience in the park? Our visit to the park and the rides we choose are driven by our desires. You have no doubt heard of the term "old souls and young souls." Even though all souls are eternal, souls that have many desires to fulfill within matter are likely to be relatively young or new to the park. If they are bored with the park and ready to move on, then chances are that they are older souls who have been around for many lifetimes. "Been there, done that" would be their motto and you would see them looking for the exit to the park rather than lining up to go on the next ride. In other words, humans are here in the park to collect a certain amount of experience, just as the soul had done previously by taking birth in the lower species.

THE RULES OF THE PARK ❧

Just like in school, you can go forward and skip grades or flunk out of the human class and go backward, that is to say downward, for some time. Thus the Vedic theory of karma does not lend itself to a New Age interpretation, in which the soul only moves upward, learning lesson after lesson. Devolution instead of evolution is also possible. If a human acts like an animal, he or she can slide back into an animal body for some time before going further forward. After all, once we are humans, we start flying our own airplanes through choice and then reap the results of our choices. If we choose to act like an animal, the message we send to Nature is: "Put me in an animal body." If you were the owner of a huge amusement park, your job would be to see to it that the park ran smoothly as well as to provide a good time for the customers. In the park of Material Nature, there are rules that govern the operation of the park, and those rules are mandatory for all the visitors.

CHAPTER 2

THE LAW OF CAUSALITY

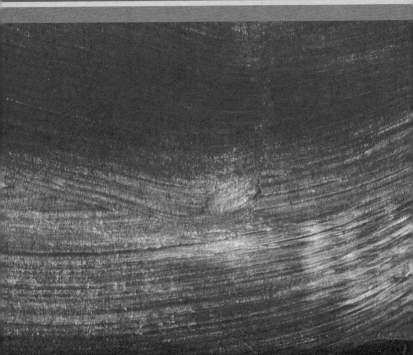

The Law

of Causality

Human actions, once imparted,
cannot be thwarted.

No one disputes that there are laws of material nature. The first and most insistent of them, gravity, has us in its grip every moment of our lives. Every situation, every object, every transaction we experience is fraught with dos and don'ts or rules of how to do something the "right" way. In matter, if we don't do it the right way, it doesn't work. Just try filling your gas tank with water and sugar instead of gasoline. In this and a myriad of other situations, there are right and wrong ways to do everything.

THE RITAM IS THE LAWS OF NATURE ❧

The English word *right* comes from the Sanskrit word *ritam*. *Ritam* simply means the invisible laws of material nature. The cosmic do's and don'ts, so to speak. The other English word derived from *ritam* is *ritual*. Doing something right is actually a series of steps or procedures. It is a ritualized way of acting that produces a predictable and desired result, conforming to the invisible laws of nature. The result of whatever you do is its karma or outcome. Remember *kri*—"to do"? While we are within matter, whatever we do produces reactions that were initiated by our use of free will. Extending that principle, the reactions of all our actions belong to and come back to us.

THE UNIVERSAL COMPUTER ❧

Since the discovery of computers and wireless communication, this ancient understanding that everything in nature is invisibly connected in a web of laws or rules has become much more obvious to us. For the moment, think of all of nature as a great mainframe computer with all of us as independent nodes with our own hard disk and processor. We are wirelessly connected to the mainframe in a kind of "inner-net." We are uploading and downloading information all the time. Right at this moment, some file that you created is downloading to you and "you have mail." The biological functions of our bodies are being conducted by a larger program of rules and regulations that exist as software in the mainframe. We are never independent of that larger system, even if we ignore its messages for some time. Ignoring the mainframe is never in our best interest and inevitably leads us to the nearest body shop to be looked at by the "body nerds" we call doctors.

RULE-BASED THINKING AND COSMIC LAW ✻

Light, air, food, electricity, various frequencies—from the obvious to the parts too small to see, packets of highly organized information are being exchanged by all the nodes on this great network of cause and effect. All of this data flow is being conducted by a rule-based system the sages of India called the *ritam*. If you ignore those rules or oppose them, your life will begin to break down. Your car will break down; your body will break down. It is for this reason that ignorance is not bliss. The simple equation for humans is "ignorance of the laws of nature = suffering." Thus, if you add the letter *m* to the Sanskrit word *ritam*, it becomes *mritam* or death. Just break all the rules all the time and see what happens—mritam.

WHY JUSTICE IS BLIND ✻

The result is death or simply failure of whatever enterprise we may be attempting. If you don't believe me, just buy a new car and then violate all the rules in the driver's manual. In no time the car will be ruined. Now I'm not suggesting that you actually go do that. The point is, karma is very strict. This is the reason that justice is portrayed as a woman holding a balance while wearing a blindfold. The woman is Mother Material Nature. The scale means that nature is always seeking balance or justice. But she is blindfolded because the laws of karma are equally applicable to everyone. Once you grasp that the eternal souls have come into matter, which is conducted by strict laws, and that upon reaching human life they are held accountable for all their actions, then the importance of karma as an understanding of life's process becomes clear.

THE COSMIC INVESTMENT PROGRAM ❧

Another metaphor for this system of cause and effect and how it influences our every action is to see karma as a financial arrangement. From this perspective, the whole of nature is a great bank in which all wealth is deposited. Humans have free will, which is an endowment of capital they receive by being eternal and conscious. Through the investing of their money (free will) in various actions and enterprises, they earn interest, receive payments, establish savings accounts, and open investments that eventually yield their ROI (return on investment) at various future dates. This means, of course, that reincarnation is an ongoing process of paying debts and receiving the profits on our portfolios of investments. We wouldn't want it to be any other way. If you work for two weeks, you expect to receive a paycheck. The problem is, the same law that gives you your pay also holds you accountable for breaking any of the rules of the system. There is no way to have free will without having both positive and negative consequences from its use.

WE ARE FARMERS PLANTING THE SEEDS OF KARMA ❧

Another way to contemplate karma is to view yourself as a farmer planting seeds. The things we do are seeds that, once planted, begin to grow. Since we are constantly acting in a variety of ways, our gardens become very complicated. In this view, our body is called the "field of activities." Since the mind and body are closely connected, even our thoughts are powerful actions that set processes in motion within our body. Whatever we eat, contact, or associate with sets waves of cause and effect rippling into motion in our bodies. To continue the agricultural metaphor, our actions plant the seeds of plants whose fruit we will reap as crops of pleasure and pain sometime in the future. Of course, this also means that whatever field (body) you currently have is also the result of many actions you planted in a previous life. How many lives ago? Who knows, but since we are eternal, that would depend on what you had planted and how long it would take to be ready to harvest (experience). In this way, if you follow the logic of karma as the continual unfolding of cause and effect that was initiated by our use of free will, then we are always reaping and sowing new actions in every moment.

WE CREATE OUR OWN HEAVEN AND HELL

The final factor in this process is the vast number of beings around us, especially the humans who also have free will. At any moment, humans may use their free will to force us to open new karmic accounts with them. It is no wonder that life in the material world is complicated. There are so many visitors to the park, and even though there are rules that govern the park in the long run, humans can use their free will in the short term to create considerable chaos in their own and everyone else's life. Thus it is that we can create heaven or hell on Earth by working cooperatively with the ritam or going against its inviolable rules. This applies to us as individuals, families, societies, and countries, and as a planet. Karma adds up and extends to every level of life on our planet.

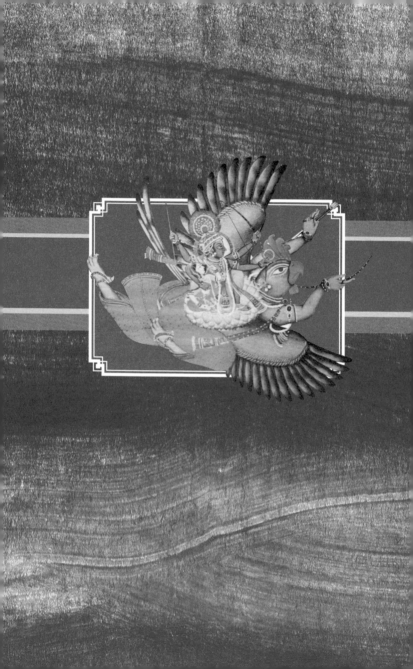

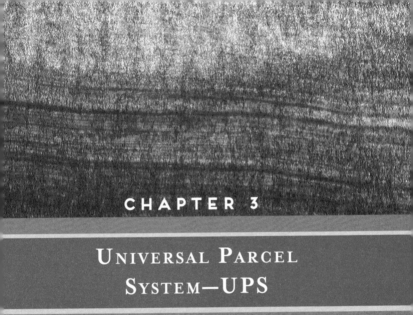

CHAPTER 3

UNIVERSAL PARCEL
SYSTEM—UPS

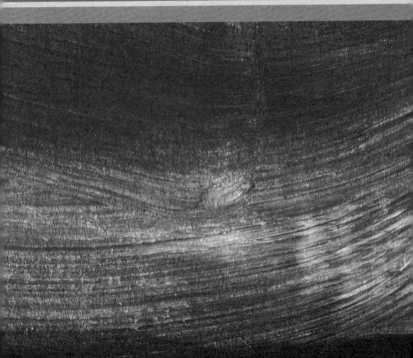

Universal Parcel

System—UPS

*You are either a deva
or have deviated in some way.*

Of all existing species, humans appear to be the only ones who ask the questions of who they are and where they come from. To answer these questions, many different religions and philosophies have arisen over time. Although there are many differences between them, they share some commonalities that show up repeatedly. One of the views found in almost every culture is that there are divine helpers, angels, or elves. They are called by these and many other names. In the Vedic literature and tradition, these divine beings are called *devas* and *devis* (since they are both male and female). The English word divine is derived from the Sanskrit *deva*, meaning "playing in the light."

Returning to the metaphor of the material world as a great amusement park, think of the devas as those beings who are acting in various roles for the purpose of maintaining the park. Sometimes these beings are also called gods because they have power over certain departments of nature, but the word "god" is misleading since it could imply that they are various competing "Gods." That is not the correct understanding of the devas. They do not compete but rather cooperate to control the flow of all natural resources. It is exactly like the city in which you live. Someone is in charge of the water department, the electricity, the gas, and the garbage collection. They are persons just like you except they are temporarily in charge of a resource that everyone needs and uses.

DEVAS HAVE LONGER LIVES ❧

So it is with the Vedic notion of the devas. They are described as souls like us or those in animals or trees, except that their current birth has given them the chance to experience being divine helpers in the cosmic park. Instead of being tourists in the park (like we humans are) they are helping to run the park, working directly with the Park Promoter. Some devas have come to that position from the transcendental realm and others have first been human. As humans, they somehow earned the right to become a deva through their good actions. Devas are said to live longer than humans and have very sublime and pleasurable lives. The creation of the devic realm precedes the creation of humans and other creatures since their functions of maintaining the park are interwoven into the laws of nature. It is written that our year is their day. Three hundred sixty of our years is their year, and multiplying by 100 equals their lifespan which then is 3,600 years. After completing their lives as devas, they also die and take their next birth as evolved humans. The angels or devas live in a place in between the earthly level and the transcendental realm. They have subtle bodies that are not directly visible to the human senses, although the devas can make themselves visible if they choose to. They are still within the material realm but are working directly in association with the Supreme Being, as the deputed managers of universal affairs.

PARKS AND RECREATION DEPARTMENT ❧

The devas work directly for the owner of the park. Whoever or whatever that Supreme Being is, the devas or angels are working directly for the Cosmic Parks and Recreation department, controlling weather and other natural processes. Of course, modern science has depersonalized all of these actions of divine intelligence into impersonal laws of nature. Remember, from the karmic point of view, both the law and the lawmaker are necessary for a complete understanding of all that exists. This means that behind every scientific process is also the personal being, or deva, managing a department of nature. Both are true at the same time. From our point of view, the devas look like processes in nature. From their point of view, we look like tourists in their park.

The devas are crucial to the understanding of karma, since they are the delivery system for our long-forgotten parcels of karma. For the moment, just imagine that whatever you do is transformed into an envelope, package, or truckload of something that belongs to you. It has your name on it. Our nature as humans is to be so busy and self-preoccupied that we easily forget our past. Just as we forget our dreams from day to day, so we forget or often would like to forget our past actions.

But if there is no cosmic accountability, then there is really no cosmic justice and no continuum of free will. If that is the case, our short-term human justice would be a foolish notion. If there is no long-term cosmic justice, then why would we, who are living within the cosmos, invent a concept of justice, and what would it be based upon? We all begin our lives in different positions of advantage or disadvantage. If this is our only life, then that is unjust. If we only live for one life, then the only conclusion is that life is unjust and unfair. How can we expect everyone to be accountable to a set of laws when they don't have equal opportunity to follow them? Such a system would be injustice parading as justice. So karma theory holds that since we are eternal individuals, as soon as we become humans, everything we do creates a stream of karma packets, letters, and packages with our names on them, which are constantly being "returned to sender."

The Vedas inform us that the devas are also the cosmic postal workers whose job it is to deliver humans their parcels of karma. We of course have usually forgotten the action that created a particular reaction. We don't know that winning the lottery probably gives us our old money back from a previous life. We can call the devas UPS, the Universal Parcel Service. Remember, accountability means you must also have an accounting system. Most people believe in accountability because it helps them to get what they want. But if the universal intelligence believes in accountability, then we are responsible for everything we do within the material world. According to the Vedas, the devas are the divine accountants and the delivery system for all our trillions of karmic packages. FedEx could learn a lot from the devas.

Now this is where karma really gets interesting. In order for the delivery system to work efficiently, the many souls in the park have to be brought together again and again in various situations in order to pay back old karmic debts to each other. This is true even though they may have forgotten their connections with each other in previous births. Whoever you may be in this life bears no obvious resemblance to who you were in your previous lives. We are not the body or mind. We are the soul. The devas remember our history even when we forget. They are the continuity between our various lives. So as it turns out, not only are the devas UPS, they are also air traffic control.

AIR TRAFFIC CONTROL ❧

Air traffic control means that, unknown to us, the devas sometimes need to control our actions in order to position us next to someone with whom we have old karma to pay or receive. These would be parents, children, spouses, coworkers, enemies, and the like. All of the inexplicable and unavoidable coincidences, accidents, or enforced circumstances in our lives are the actions of the devic air traffic control department. At this point we can hear the human voice saying, "But, but what about my free will?" Of course, my friends, free will is how we created the results that UPS and air traffic control are kindly delivering to us. They are ensuring that over time there truly is cosmic justice. Even when we move to another body, they know our forwarding address.

THOUGHTS PUT THE WHEELS IN MOTION 🌱

The question of free will is always at the center of any discussion of karma. In order to understand free will better, we need to take a closer look at exactly what action (or *doing*) is for us as humans. According to the Vedic theory, there are three kinds of doing that generate karmic reactions: thinking, speaking, and acting through our body. All three of these uses of our free will start the wheels of karmic reaction turning in some way.

The first and most subtle of our actions is thinking. The Vedic saying is, "Everything rests upon desire." It is described that our mind is the place of contact between us and the devas. They can hear or smell our thoughts and desires and begin responding to them in real time. In other words, they are directly hearing what we think and feel. Just envision your mind as a wireless connector, a kind of cell phone, and whatever you could have, be, or do in the park as something you request from the devas, just like ordering from a catalog. In this way, thoughts and desires are received by the devas as your request to have that particular item delivered or to deliver you to where that item is. Hence, the saying "be careful what you wish for." In a similar way, every cell in your body "hears" your every thought and it reacts immediately through the mind-body link. What we think directly begins to reprogram our biocomputer. Thoughts are also picked up by other beings exactly in the way information from cell phones or wireless internet is sent and received. Just by thinking we are doing.

WORDS CAN BE BINDING ❀

Next come words. Our speech is more powerful than we can imagine. In most cultures on our planet, until recent times, a person's word was binding. All agreements were verbal. One's word was one's bond. Therefore the things we say put energies in motion that become reality. We literally speak things into manifestation. If you speak badly of others, you are cursing them. If you speak kindly of them, you are blessing them. Perhaps the image of the little devil on one shoulder and deva or angel on the other is not so far-fetched. By speaking, we create lasting impressions of who we are on all of those around us. These impressions create our futures. We have all experienced situations in life where words were spoken that put very powerful actions into motion. Sometimes words can be withdrawn and forgiven, but at other times, just by speaking, we set an irrevocable course of action in motion.

As for actions, they are the last irreversible step. Sometimes we can erase or undo thoughts or even words, but actions are the request for the pizza that, once ordered, cannot be sent back. The truck has left the building and the devas are about to deliver something you ordered in the now forgotten past. If

you are delivered something unpleasant, you could say, "Poor me, I am a victim," or if you receive something wonderful you could say, "Lucky me, I did something right." In either case, whatever lands, in spite of your current desires or wishes, is a parcel of karma you ordered by acting in the past. If you don't accept that it was created by your own action, then it can only have been imposed by some unknown Being or force, in which case we are consigned to being perpetual victims of blind destiny.

In the karmic view, we are always in a position to play the game better and by so doing change the outcome. The rules of action and reaction are obviously running the park; science has demonstrated that clearly for everyone to understand. Once you add our eternal nature into the equation, the result is long-term action and reaction with free will and personal accountability. Our dilemma is that the size of the universe seems daunting to our minds. We have trouble imagining that any system of accounting could be so complex and accurate. We are inclined to underestimate the Divine Intelligence.

ALL THE WORLD IS A STAGE ✤

In the final analysis, this view of karma should broaden our view of life considerably. We are souls evolving by trial and error in a vast university that is managed from top to bottom by invisible divine intelligence. Nonetheless, our free will is running the show, even though the balance is always being maintained by divine law and the constant efforts of the devas. As for us as humans, Shakespeare got it right when he said, "All the world is a stage and the men and women are merely players." Whatever we appear to be now does not at all resemble the thousand previous births that came before. Yet according to Vedic karma theory, all those births and this one as well have created and continue to create a stream of reactions that are the by-product of being in the world of matter. We are truly souls having a human experience, while the devas are souls having a heavenly material experience. But all the souls are playing at being something they are not, on the big stage of the material world. We are all in costumes made of matter. From microbes to plants to animals to humans to devas, all are eternal souls dressed in matter.

CHAPTER 4

KARMA, DEATH, AND DYING

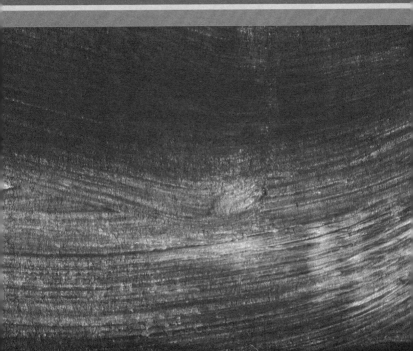

Karma,

Death, and Dying

What you resist persists,
what you fear draws near.

As we have seen, by its very nature the empirical scientific methodology is not designed to answer spiritual or materially unverifiable questions. That is because its process demands a repeatable experiment for separate validation of a theory. The strength of material science is technology within matter. Its weakness is that our senses, even aided by scientific equipment, can only see so far. Beyond that point we cannot directly perceive reality. If empirical scientists insist that nothing is true beyond that point, they become priests in their own religion instead of the material technicians that they should be according to their own methodology. Empirical science does not have any special authority or qualification to speak on what is beyond the materially provable. In spite of this, in our popular culture the authority of empirical science often extends beyond the areas of its actual knowing. To the untrained mind, knowledge in one discipline creates an air of authority in other unrelated disciplines. For the same reason, we ask movie stars their opinion on many things that they have no proper qualifications to answer.

KARMA THEORY ORIGINATES IN THE VEDAS ✻

The theory of karma as taught in the Vedas of India presents itself as a body of insight into the workings of the material universe and what is beyond. Some of what it teaches is materially verifiable, like any scientific matter, and some of it is meant to be the subject of meditation by us. In the study of karma, scientific knowledge and empirically unverifiable knowledge are both present. This chapter is devoted to the process of death. It is based on descriptions from the Vedas that attempt to convey some idea of what takes place when we make the transition from one body to the next in our continued transmigration around the Ferris wheel of samsara. Rather than thinking of these descriptions as literal, like a science textbook, think of them as a poetic or metaphorical attempt to convey some of the subtle processes that take place when we leave one body and transition to another through the divine guidance of the devas.

The first thing to remember is that the devas are mediating or assisting in all of the transitions, even when we may be unconscious or unaware. Remember that the amusement park is open 24/7, also when we are asleep or unconscious. It is just like any big city. Whether you are awake or asleep, the water, electricity, garbage, street signals, and police and fire departments are all still working. Similarly, the divine helpers are always awake whether we notice them or not. With this in mind, let's hear what the Vedas have to say about how we go from one body to another.

THE DENSE AND SUBTLE BODIES ❧

In order to understand how death works, we need to look more closely at the *gu* (remember the goo?) that surrounds our souls as our mind-body complex. According to karma theory, we actually have two bodies: One is a dense physical body made of heavy matter. That body is made up of the five great elements, earth, water, fire, air, and space, which are further broken down into the 108 or so atomic elements of modern perception. This is the dense body we are used to using as our vehicle in the material world, though some people think of it as their actual "self." Within or beyond that body is a subtle covering made up of mind, intelligence, and egoic conceptions of self. That subtle body is the same one we become during dreams. While dreaming, even though our physical body is parked on the bed, we continue to be active in our subtle body. Underneath both of those coverings we find our true self as the jiva-atma or soul.

These two bodies, the dense and subtle, are coverings over our true selves. Thus it is often said that the physical body is our coat, the subtle body is our shirt, and our naked body is like the pure soul with no material coverings. With this in mind you could say that dreaming is running around the cosmos in your nightshirt. Of course the three (body, mind, and soul) are connected once we take birth within the material world. It is said that whatever we experience from life to life is recorded on our subtle bodies. We are bar-coded with all the things we do and we carry the record of our past with us wherever we travel and from birth to birth. In addition, many things that are recorded in our subtle bodies as memories are reflected into our physical bodies as outward expressions of our inner states. That is the mind-body link. Recently the science of massage therapy and bodywork such as Rolfing, Bowen, cranial-sacral, chiropractic, and many others have acknowledged that what is stored in the subtle body is often stored in the physical body as well.

LORD YAMA AND THE COURT OF KARMIC JUSTICE ✤

The devas know that each soul has an allotment of time in a particular body. When that time is up, the devas send a few of their own workers to collect us—that is, to remove us from our physical bodies. This experience we call death. Think of those angels/devas as representatives of the cosmic judicial system. They usually have to drag us out of whatever we are doing in the physical world because of our intense attachment to the physical realm. According to some descriptions in the Vedas, the devas throw a net over our subtle bodies and pull us out of our physical bodies. We are then transported from there to a special part of the devic realm that is devoted to death and rebirth. You could think of it as the cosmic courthouse. This is where Mother Nature keeps the scales that measure and balance all we do or have done.

As you can well imagine, this process is very disorienting to most souls since they were very attached to their previous material lives. A transition period follows, during which their bodies are cremated or buried, and they are mourned and memorialized by those who knew them. Finally they end up as faint memories. But to the devas, the deceased are eternal souls who need to continue their evolution within the realms of matter. So after some time, souls, who are still wearing the nightshirts of the subtle body, are calmed and pacified. Finally, when their turns come, they are taken into the courtroom of cosmic justice to evaluate their last lives and learn of their next ones.

In the Vedas, this entire process is described in considerable detail. The deva in charge of this process is named Yamaraja, or the Lord of Death and Judgment. He is the administrator of the ritam, or universal laws. His assistant is named Chitragupta, the court recorder. All that he records is kept in a vast library which you may have heard of; it is called the Akashic records. *Akasha* refers to the element space. The idea here is that all our thoughts, words and deeds are observed and recorded by other higher intelligences that are monitoring our long-term spiritual evolution.

THE DEVAS DO NOT FORGET ❧

At this point, the subtle body of the soul is examined and the nuances of cause and effect are explained to the soul. You could say in modern terms that the soul is shown the movie of its life and the subtle concepts of cosmic law of cause and effect are explained to him. Think of this as an educational process rather than a judgmental or punitive one. After all, some souls receive very good news at that meeting and are told of the wonderful progress they are making. Others receive not such great news as the result of things they have done to harm others or cause great pain. All of this is just the movie of what we chose to do. And the devas do not forget, or rather, they can read what we carry with us in our subtle bodies. According to the Vedic report on this, we are in their hands entirely once we are no longer in a physical body.

In the final step of this process, the soul is told of its future. To simplify this, imagine again that our use of free will is a constant process of investment. We could say that this meeting of the atma with Yamaraja and Chitragupta is a kind of meeting with your banker and accountant, who then tell you how much money you have available to spend for the next year (that is, in your next life). They tell you who your next parents will be, your siblings and relations, how much money you will have coming, and your gender and type of body, as well as many other predetermined details.

After that consultation, you will be readied for transition to the next womb. After nine months or so you will reemerge in another physical body (assuming you have come back as human again). You will still be the same soul with the same subtle body, filled with impressions from previous lives, but once you are born all of that will lie below the surface to unfold gradually in your new life. Picture the moment of your birth, metaphorically speaking, when the deva airplane lands (that stork we always heard about) and you are handed to your parents as their new bundle of joy. Unknown to them, your suitcases full of karmas from previous lives are stored in the basement. On them is a sign that says, "Open these when you leave home and start to use free will again."

Most societies don't hold children responsible for their actions with the same degree of culpability as they do adults. Of course, for us humans, free will does start at a fairly young age. In no time we will be making choices that again create new reactions that will become our future. And most likely, that bully who always tormented you was a reincarnated player from your past in some forgotten previous life. The same is true for your parents, siblings, relatives, and teachers. Only the Supreme Being and the devas know the secrets of our karmic past, though a good psychic or astrologer can gain some insight into the things that are in our karmic suitcases. That is because some of those karmas are already cued up for delivery. As you have probably suspected by now, there are various kinds of karmas and the whole subject is as complex as any elaborate legal system, only this legal jurisdiction is conducted on a cosmic scale for trillions of souls.

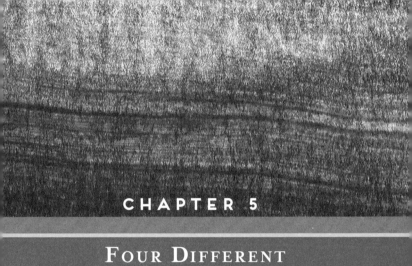

CHAPTER 5

FOUR DIFFERENT TYPES OF KARMA

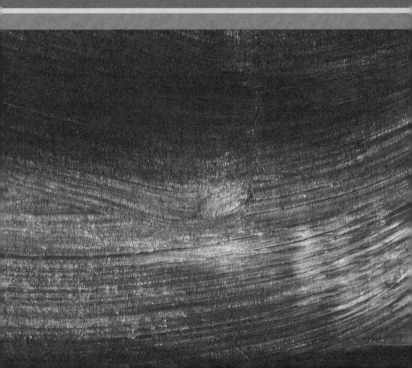

Four Different

Types of Karma

*Intention is the engine
of action.*

Almost all the ancient cultures of the world believed in concepts very similar to the atma, karma, and reincarnation. A rose by any other name would smell the same. Our modern ignorance of or resistance to karma got its start when the Western Catholic Church passed a resolution at a fifth-century Nicene council, stating that in their view the soul did not exist before the body. By that vote, opposition to karma and reincarnation became Catholic dogma and have been taught as such ever since.

That dogma was then also passed on to most of the Protestant branches of Christianity as well.

Before the teachings on an eternal soul and reincarnation were voted out of the Catholic doctrine, many devout Christians of the first four centuries had believed that reincarnation was the actual true understanding of Jesus's teachings. The Roman Catholic view finally prevailed and the concept of rebirth was generally referred to by them as the "Eastern Heresy." The departure from viewing the soul as eternal did later cause some considerable philosophical problems for the Catholic theologians. Since Catholics are required to be baptized at birth for the removal of their sins, the more observant among them began to ask some difficult questions. If the soul did not exist before the body, they reasoned, then how could it have sinned? If it had only existed as a baby, what sins could it possibly have committed?

ORIGINAL SIN INVENTED ✤

This caused the sixth-century Catholic theologian Augustine to invent an explanation for this dilemma called "Original Sin." He explained the story of Adam and Eve as a drama in which the woman tempted the man to eat the apple (have sex). They were then thrown out of the garden for that indiscretion, by an angry God. Later, their sin was somehow passed on to their children, a sort of early precursor to genetics. In this view then, although the soul did not exist before sex, it somehow came into being through sex, and the sin of being born by sex made the soul evil enough to require baptism for purification. In this way, the subject of reincarnation was temporarily avoided. There was also no attempt to define the difference between consciousness in animals or plants and in people. Why are people conscious with a soul whereas animals are also conscious yet have no soul? Where does their consciousness arise from? These and many other philosophical questions are related to reincarnation as an explanation of life.

For the last 1,500 years, the Catholic and Protestant churches have remained entrenched in this fifth-century decision. In the same way that science was persecuted, so have views like reincarnation been maligned and labeled as heresy, even though they are the most ancient spiritual teachings of our planet and also support a grand view of both individuality and divine justice. Some people think that the Nicene councils were trying to take power over common people by telling them they only have one lifetime. This tactic is well-known in the world of business as the "impending doom close." The salesman says: "Act now folks, because the sale ends tomorrow."

In other words, if I tell you that you are not divine and are a sinner and that I alone can grant you immortality, that gives me absolute power over your life and future. In the Vedic teaching, we are all souls, and consciousness is the symptom of the soul's existence in a plant, human, or animal. No one can grant you immortality, since it is already your very nature.

THE BIG VIEW IS REINCARNATION ❋

The Vedic view is that an eternal soul, cosmic justice, and reincarnation are the teachings that honor the individual the most and offer a big view of our potential to evolve as divine beings over long periods of time. Reincarnation also

removes the rush to judge the soul and send it to hell or heaven after only one lifetime. If being judged for our actions is an ongoing process, then from life to life we are always in some condition that is a response to our previous actions. We are the drivers of our own karma.

Returning to our discussion of the types of karma performed by the souls, we are constantly engaged in various kinds of actions. This means that a steady stream of reactions will necessarily follow what we think, speak, and do. Those reactions are categorized differently according to the degree of ripeness of the fruits of our deeds. For the moment, think like a farmer observing the various crops you have planted in your fields.

RIPE FRUIT KARMA ✸

The first kind of karma to consider is called *prarabda* in Sanskrit and means "ripe fruit." If you have ever picked fruit, you know that when it is ripe, the fruit falls into your hand by simply touching it. If it is unripe, it stays on the tree. The first ripe-fruit karma we received this lifetime was our body, and with it our parents and extended family. This includes our genetic code and whatever problems and advantages come with that particular combination of factors. *Prarabda karma* is also called *destiny*, or *manifest karma*. It is the part of our reality that we cannot change by exerting any amount of free will.

Later on, if you decide to have children, whichever ones are delivered by the devas will be yours. You cannot send them back. Aside from these biological givens, most of our childhood circumstances that are beyond our control— teachers, school, classmates, our parents' relationship, their longevity, childhood diseases, and many more circumstances—

are all prarabda karmas. In addition to those, there is a certain number of events or experiences that the devas are scheduled to deliver to us at a specific time in any lifetime.

We are usually unaware of the devas' delivery schedule and of the necessity of our receiving whatever they must deliver. After all, they are just giving us the things we have previously created by the use of our free will. There is the saying, "If the universe gives you lemons, make lemonade." For "universe," just think of the devas who are delivering your karma on behalf of the Supreme Being, the owner of the park. Then again, you may as easily have cherries delivered instead of lemons. It all depends on your unseen but very real karmic history.

SEEDLING KARMA ✤

The second variety of karma is called *sanchitta*, or the seeds of karma that are contained in our subtle bodies. Changing our bodies is very difficult to understand and at some levels impossible. Yet it is our destiny and therefore unchangeable. But changing our minds is an everyday, moment-to-moment process that we understand. It is conducted by free will, or at least it could be. The Vedic definition of "mind" is "that organ of cognition that performs the activities of thinking, feeling, and willing." Just as there is a tendency for us to think we are our bodies, calling the bodies our selves, so we have an even greater tendency to identify our minds as our selves. The philosopher Descartes said it very clearly: "I think, therefore I am." The Vedic view however is that we are the atma, and both mind and body are the coverings of matter. If the body is made up of sticky pieces of *gu* (goo) that we have accumulated by eating, drinking, and breathing, then what is the mind made of? What are its contents and how do they affect us?

The simple answer is memories of past experience. These memories can be of this lifetime or of many previous lifetimes. In that sense, each person is like an archeological dig, with layer after layer of past experience encoded into his or her subtle body. A useful way to think of the dense body and subtle body is to compare them to a computer and its software. Our bodies, the computers, come with certain capabilities hardwired into their constructions, and our subtle bodies come loaded with the software downloaded through previous life experiences and acquired abilities.

Previously experienced emotions are also embedded in each person's subtle body, along with a large number of programs that have been placed there by parenting, social pressure, and our own intentional learning. Along with those various programs are also old habits of thinking in certain patterns. The Vedas state it this way: "Habit is our second nature." Our first nature is the soul, or atma, but certain patterns in our subtle bodies that are the residue of our past karma continue to control our future actions. Unless those patterns are changed, we will continue to repeat the same actions again and again. We are both preprogrammed and reprogrammable.

For this reason, our subtle bodies are the places where current desires, past impressions, and habitual patterns grow like seeds. Technically speaking, those mental seeds do not have to grow into a destiny or irrevocable future if they are removed in time. This "changing our mind" is the primary aim of yoga and a variety of other Vedic arts of modifying our future by changing or reprogramming the software in the subtle body. Sanchitta karma can be altered by the use of free will. Just like changing an old habit, the mind can have old files removed from the subtle body. The result will then be a different way of doing and thus a different future destiny.

CREATING OUR FUTURE FROM PRESENT ACTIONS ❧

The third variety of karma consists of the results from our current actions. If prarabda karma is the destined events we cannot prevent and sanchitta karma is the seeds of future action sitting upon the subtle body, then the third variety of karma is called *agama karma*, the karma being generated by our current actions. It has been said that there is one radio station that everyone in the world is always listening to: "What's In It for Me?"

The Vedas call this *ahamkara* or "material ego." The dilemma for us is that we are filled with desires for the experiences within the park, but we are not always very mindful about the effect our actions are having on the whole system and those around us. In this regard, the devas can be compared to the ecology department. They have control over the weather, the resources of nature, and the ebb and flow of all other species as part of their work in maintaining the park. But we humans with our extreme free will are the wild card in the deck. We can upset the balance of nature with our tendency to want more and more. To quote Mahatma Gandhi, "The Lord has provided enough for everyone's need. He has not provided enough for everyone's greed." Our current actions can take the ecological viewpoint of the devas into consideration, or we can use our free will to override their attempts at restoring balance to the world around us.

Even though we have destined limitations and a residual set of abilities and habitual ideas, at any given moment we can make life-altering decisions with the use of free will. Some of those decisions will shape the unfolding of events in our current lives, as obvious reactions to what we choose, while the larger number of reactions to what we do will be deposited into or debited from our future karma accounts. All existing possibilities for changing our positions and locations within the park result from the conscious choices we are making in the present moment.

THE LAW OF ASSOCIATION ✺

That present moment can be run on autopilot from past habits of mind, our sanchitta karma, or we can reassert our conscious choices to dramatically redirect our destinies in the present moment. The secret of agama karma lies in two things. The first is that whatever we associate with, we

become like. We become like what we like. Not only is the *gu* sticky and all around us, it also has particular qualities that either improve us or degrade us. We all know that children need good role models in order not to become bad citizens. Good or bad, there are states within matter that are either destructive, and agitating, or peaceful and balanced. There is an old Chinese proverb that says, "Your parents are chosen for you, your siblings are chosen for you, your spouse is chosen for you, your children are chosen for you, so the only thing you get to choose is your friends." In a very real sense, our future karma is created by the alliances and friendships we choose with free will in the present moment. From those associations will come actions of a particular type which will determine our future.

TAKING A VOW ❧

The second secret of agama karma is called *vrata* in Sanskrit. Vrata means "taking a vow." Because humans do not have a purely instinctual nature like other creatures, we are forced to decide who and what we are by choosing among the many choices life constantly offers. That decision-making requires that we define our selves and our boundaries of action. This is the tension of human life that distinguishes us from all other births. We can choose to dive back into the animal kingdom, or we can choose to become a deva, or divine helper, though they must eventually return as a human. We can remain human and by so doing involve our selves in some enterprise of action that will define our futures. Finally we may follow some path that leads us back to the spiritual and transcendental realm from which we originally set forth on this journey. In every case, to maintain any path, we must finally take a vow and stick to it, in order to be self-defining in

the creation of our futures. Our current vows, or the lack of them, are defining who our friends are, and between them our next future is being created as our agama karma.

ACTION WITHOUT KARMA

The last major category of karma could be described as "no karma." Remember the concept of old souls vs. young souls? If we have come to this world to explore and learn, then our karmas are how we steer our ships from one place to another within the park. But what happens when a soul finishes with the park and is ready to leave? Let's just say for the purposes of this discussion that the Vedas describe this material world as having an entrance coming in from the transcendental world and also an exit back out to the transcendental world. You will know you are an old soul when playing in the park no longer excites you, but the prospect of finding the exit gives you great enthusiasm. This process of finally exiting the material world is called *moksha* in Sanskrit. In English, we could call it "final liberation," or the return of the atma to its original home from which the journey into the dark realm of matter began.

Of course, the journey from young soul to old soul is usually a gradual process over many lifetimes. *Kriyamana karma,* then, is something we accumulate from life to life through our various spiritual activities. This so-called karma is fundamentally different from material karma in that kriyamana karma, once earned, is never lost or exhausted. It accumulates from life to life until we are ready to graduate from the university. All other karmas are temporary responses to our egocentric actions. You invest money, win a million dollars, spend it, and then it is gone forever. But with kriyamana karma, certain kinds of special actions build an account of "liberation karma." That account is never diminished. In chapter 7, we will examine this process of final liberation in more detail.

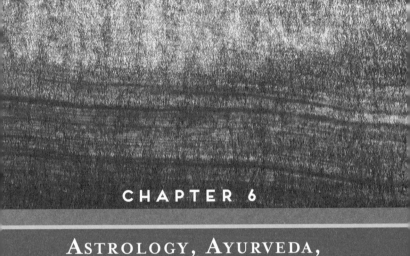

CHAPTER 6

ASTROLOGY, AYURVEDA, AND THE SCIENCE OF KARMA

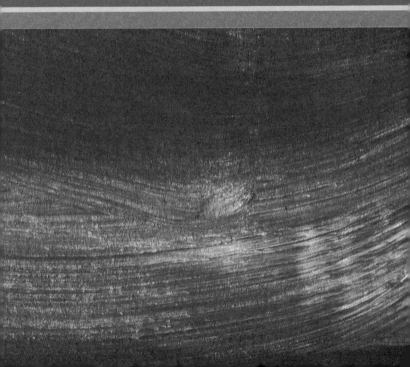

Astrology, Ayurveda,

and the Science of Karma

Mind is the soul's cocoon,
body is the branch it is attached to.

In modern times, the great and ancient science of astronomy/astrology has been misunderstood, maligned, and often made into trivial entertainment for consumption in the daily newspaper. In spite of the recent decline of astrology under the criticism of both modern science and various religions, it remains of interest to billions of people throughout the world. In its entertainment form it is a multi-billion-dollar industry. In the West, astrology also has a long history. When astrology was not being persecuted by church or state, as recently as two hundred years ago it was taught at medical schools as a sister science of medicine. It has been studied and used regularly by some of the greatest leaders and thinkers in world history.

But long before modern times, be it the early days of Christianity, the Roman Empire, or even Greek culture, astrology was practiced in India under the name of *Jyotisha*. This name means "the science of how light regulates life." In the last fifty years, along with various forms of yoga, Ayurvedic medicine and many other branches of Vedic learning, Jyotisha has spread around the world and is now sometimes called Hindu astrology, or more correctly, Vedic astrology. Jyotisha has always been associated with the Vedic knowledge and culture of India. As in the later medical schools of Europe, Vedic astrology and the medical system of India called Ayurveda were always considered sister sciences. Both medicine and astrology in India are based upon the principles of soul, karma, and reincarnation.

AYURVEDA, THE MEDICAL SYSTEM OF ANCIENT INDIA ❧

Ayurveda is the science of preserving life whereas modern allopathic medicine is mostly concerned with treating diseases or emergency conditions after they have arisen. Ayurveda was primarily concerned with the prevention of the imbalances in lifestyle and diet that lead to disease. Secondarily, Ayurveda had also developed very advanced surgical procedures. Only modern medicine has excelled beyond what Ayurveda had achieved. By 800 BCE, Ayurveda had developed procedures for brain surgery, anesthesia, cataract operations, and reconstructive plastic surgery. Ayurveda also developed an extensive herbal and pharmacological system in which thousands of plants and substances were cataloged for medical use, many of which have been patented as modern pharmacological remedies.

In those remote times, Vedic astrology was also very sophisticated in its astronomical understanding of the universe. The Vedic system of time calculation is the only culture other than our modern technological one to calculate the age of the universe in billions of years. Indian astronomers and mathematicians were the historical source of the use of zero, the so-called Arabic numerals 1-10, calculus, trigonometry, algebra, and binary mathematics, and they had accurately calculated the motion of the Earth's wobble to precisely 25,920 years. They knew the Sun was the center of the solar system and had correctly calculated the distances between and relative sizes of the Earth, Moon, and Sun.

ASTRONOMICAL KNOWLEDGE WAS USED IN MEDICINE ✺

This considerable astronomical knowledge was applied to two principal endeavors. The first was living in harmony with the seasons and energies of the cosmos. This is crucial to Ayurvedic medicine, as it promotes harmony with nature. The second is the use of astronomical information to understand the nature, timing, and delivery of karma. In the case of Ayurveda, lunar, solar, and planetary energies surround us at all times. Those, along with seasonal influences, are the ever-changing cosmic background that we as humans need to harmonize with in order to stay balanced. Ask any traditional farmer and he or she will tell you that the success or failure of the crop depends upon the farmer's knowledge of the seasons, Moon, and Sun, as well as an understanding of weather, water, and the complex effect those forces have on all life.

For this chapter, Vedic astrology as the science of observing karma is our theme. As before, the place to begin our understanding of karma is first that it is rooted in the ritam, or invisible universal laws of nature. Second, that it is the devas who are the maintainers of nature and also the delivery mechanism for natural cause and effect. We call them the laws of nature. If you remember, the Sanskrit word *deva* means "playing in the light." Jyotisha is the science of how light is regulating all the cause and effect of life. Astrology is also called the science of time—since time is measured as the relationship between light and space—regulating the unfolding of cause and effect. Light moves at 186,000 miles per second. We could say that this is the visible speed limit in matter for the unfolding of events. The ancient thinkers saw light as the action of divine intelligence, ultimately the Supreme Being acting through the devas to regulate all life in our biosphere.

THE DEVAS ARE BEHIND THE SCENES ✤

Picture the devas as the behind-the-scenes divine agents who are constantly scheduling the delivery of all of our letters, packages, and truckloads of karma. Sometimes, in order to stay on schedule, they have to get inside our minds and whisper suggestions to us, to direct us to the correct locations where the delivery or hand-off of certain karma is to be made. To us, their suggestions feel exactly like thoughts of our own creation, since they occur within our minds. Because we think we are the mind, the suggestions of the devas look like our own thoughts and ideas.

They say, "Why don't you go to the store?" and we think, "Why don't I go to the store?" They say, "You are in love with this person," and we say, "I am in love with this person." This is the part of karma theory that drives ordinary humans crazy. Those who think we are alone here say: "What about my free will? If the devas are controlling my thoughts, then there is no free will." The Vedic answer to this important question is that the devas are only controlling our minds when they need to make a delivery of something we ordered in the past. At that moment they do a system override, suspending our free will so we will receive the results of our past actions. The rest of the time we are running either by habit or free will. One might reply, "What right do they have to be inside my head and thoughts, telling me what to do?" The answer, of course, is simple—divine right; they work for the Supreme Being who owns the park. We have volunteered to come here and once here are forced to accept the rules of the park and the results of our own actions.

This is the conceptual framework behind Vedic astrology as the main science that gives insight into our previous karmas and their delivery schedule. For detailed information on this subject, please read my recent publication, the *Vedic Astrology Deck*, also published by Mandala. The short version of the story goes as follows: Since the souls are in the devas' hands during their transition from one life to another, the devas arrange the exact moment of birth according to the large and complex number of karmic variables and deliveries that are being given to the soul in their next life. This is the "air traffic control" part of the devas' job. The exact and complex trajectories of karmic deliveries are mapped out in advance in ways that are more complex than we can easily imagine.

THE PLACE AND TIME OF BIRTH CREATE THE HOROSCOPE ✤

Thus, the exact position in the sky of stars and planets at the precise latitude and longitude of birth creates a mathematical diagram composed of the points of light in the sky. That diagram is called a horoscope or "view of the hour" of birth. It could also be called a "karma-scope" since the devas' information regarding the individual's karma, along with the delivery schedule of when it will be delivered, is secretly encoded in the patterns in the sky at the moment of birth. However far-fetched or difficult this may be to conceive, the best minds of various great cultures have consistently found empiric and observable truth in the science of astrology throughout the ages. It is even said that the scientist and philosopher Newton, who was once criticized by one of his peers for his interest in astrology, replied curtly, "Sir, I have studied these things, whereas you have not." The critics of astrology should first learn it as a science, before they pass critical judgment on what they have not studied.

Vedic astrology, like much of the ancient wisdom of India, is still intact as an unbroken tradition for over six thousand years. Both Vedic astrology and Ayurveda were traditionally used to monitor and correct manifest and soon-to-manifest karmic imbalances in all persons. A preventive Ayurvedic physician examines the body to determine where problematic cause and effect may be unfolding. According to this perspective, disease of any kind is rooted in a violation of the ritam or laws of nature. That imbalance, if uncorrected, continues to develop in seven stages, culminating in what modern medicine finally calls symptoms and labels as a disease. The final stage of incurability is simply the end of a long period of imbalance that has ended in an incurable—that is to say, irreversible—physical condition. In this way, doctors, Ayurvedic or otherwise, are involved with prarabda karma, the ripe fruit of long-term patterns of cause and effect.

VEDIC ASTROLOGY SEES THE
KARMIC HISTORY ❧

Vedic astrology sees the entire karmic history unfolding over time. Some things visible in the chart will be prarabda karmas that will happen because they must. Some karmas will show up as sanchitta, or tendencies, habits, abilities, and deficiencies that are the legacy from previous lives. Finally, some conditions will arise from temporary forces of nature that are transitory. In this area, before there was psychology, Vedic astrologers and Ayurvedic doctors worked as a team. They understood the mind-body connection. The mind influences the body, the body influences the mind, and nature influences both. This means that the early stages of a physical imbalance can often be altered by changing the thoughts and emotions, just as in the later stages, physical methods are also necessary. The horoscope reveals the inherent tendencies of the subtle body as well as temporary natural forces that are impinging upon us.

Finally, because we live within and are part of the complete matrix of cosmic energies, as they move we are affected by their motions. Some celestial bodies, like the Sun and Moon, push on us in very obvious and measurable ways. The planets' and stars' influence is more subtle. The changing patterns of cosmic energy are observed by the Vedic astrologer to understand how karmic patterns are unfolding. The question is often asked, "Do the planets impel or compel?" From the Vedic astrological, Ayurvedic, and karmic perspectives, the answer is both. Sometimes the planets compel the delivery of an old piece of cause and effect. This will be visible to the astrologer as some movement within the sky as seen in relation to the same sky at the moment of a person's birth. Otherwise, the planets may impel by creating a climate of cosmic vibration that acts to impel us just as weather does in our daily lives. The physician will observe the same forces as changing the patterns of symptoms within the body.

To make this clearer, imagine that at the moment of conception, the exact combination of each person's genetic code is formed. From that time on, and throughout our lives, that specific gene code is programming various bodily functions as well as influencing various psychological functions and abilities. In addition, with our mental attitudes, we are reprogramming the genetic hardware by downloading new software (knowledge) into our systems. Similarly, the exact picture of the sky at your birth and all the points of light measurable in the sky, contain information about our specific karmic situation. As the planets continue their orbits around the sun, they not only move through the sky, but move through our own personal horoscope. Embedded in that horoscope are thousands of bits of information about us that can be extracted by a knowledgeable Vedic astrologer and seen by a skilled Ayurvedic medical practitioner. Similarly, a skilled geneticist could know volumes about you if he could properly interpret the relations contained in your genetic code.

HOROSCOPE IS KARMA-SCOPE ✵

This is an important point. Just because astrology can be used to read your karmic patterns doesn't mean that everyone who claims to know astrology, in fact, does. We all understand that the same is true in medicine or genetics. That something can be done in theory is one thing; doing it in practice is another. Vedic astrology is a very complete presentation of the science of karma. Most systems of astrology have some truth in them but how much varies widely. The point here is "let the buyer beware." Much of modern astrology is in a state of disrepair as a science at this moment in history because it is underfunded in terms of scientific research and without paid and respectable teaching positions. In spite of that, India's Vedic astrology has kept the science alive and well with university recognition at the highest PhD level. No conversation on karma is complete without this proper understanding of the "karma-scope" or horoscope. It is the view of our cause and effect from life to life as seen by the divine intelligences of nature.

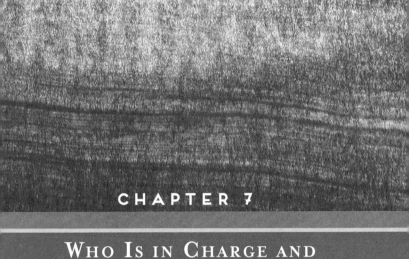

CHAPTER 7

WHO IS IN CHARGE AND HOW TO GET FREE

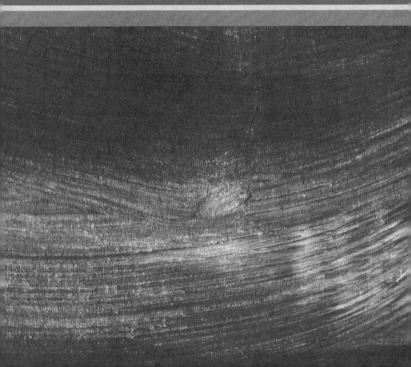

Who Is in Charge

and How to Get Free

*Beyond the wall of ignorance
is the garden of Divinity.*

Since all discussions of cause and effect are examining some aspect of karma, the subject of right and wrong action is common to every spiritual tradition. As we have seen, the critical point that opens cause and effect up to its fullest extension is the view that we as individual beings are eternal and cannot die. The Vedas teach that immortality is not something we earn or that is granted to us, but that it is our true and essential nature. We are souls whose existence stretches to eternity in both directions, past and future.

The fact of our eternal nature does not remove the tension of our situation within the material world. Even though for the purpose of our discussion, I have described our visit to the realms of matter as a visit to a divinely constructed amusement park, being in the park is often less than amusing. On the darker side of things, even though we are eternal by nature, just arriving in the park guarantees that we will forget who we truly are as we pass through the countless species of life. By the time we reach human life, the poignancy of our situation is excruciatingly painful. We see the beauty of life and are madly attracted to it and then step by step lose everything we have achieved. Even if we are fortunate enough to live a relatively happy life without tragedy or disaster, we cannot help but see the misery and suffering that exist all around us. We may be sitting happily in one part of the park but in the distance, the sirens of someone's disaster can be heard.

THE FOUR PROBLEMS OF MATERIAL LIFE ❊

The four concomitant processes that accompany us on our journeys through matter are birth, disease, old age, and death. No one in the material park is free from these inevitable and painful processes. From the smallest microbe to the mightiest deva, all have a beginning, then age, decay, and eventually are forced to leave their old and worn-out body to find yet another vehicle. Because we are eternal there is no end to this process as long as we are within matter. This samsara, or wheel of repeated birth and death, is nothing more than a reflection of the temporary nature of matter itself. Matter is unconscious and made of parts, whereas we are conscious and eternal by nature. This means that there is no permanent shelter or home for us within the material park. From top to bottom there is no place where we can stay, since even the park itself is periodically dissolved only to be rebuilt again and then again dissolved. This view is presented in the Vedas as the basis of karma.

It is our very nature that is frustrated by this process of birth, disease, aging, and death. What we want is a trouble-free, unlimited life of pleasure, creativity, and joy. But here there are only moments of what we want, while most of our life is interspersed with work, pain, suffering, depression, and unfulfilled desires.

In response to this dilemma, some philosophers promote the idea that there is a material or technological solution to our discomfort within matter. They say that we are material in our nature and that there is nothing beyond this current realm of our experience. From this conclusion, they continue with the view that there are no devas or distributed divine intelligences and ultimately no Park Promoter or Supreme Being behind the park. Thus they define the laws of nature as arbitrary and random rules which we can bend or break as we see fit or as far as is possible. The ultimate goal of this view is either a pleasurable material life for the few while pretending to wish the same for all, or an ideal of equal distribution of material resources to all. Neither of these approaches solves the ultimate problem of our distress at the very unconscious nature of matter. No political or technological solution solves the problem of death.

The opposite view sees all living beings as of the same inherent transcendental and divine nature. It sees them all here by their own choices, evolving through the species and finally into human life, as a learning process in their souls' eternal journey to understand both each other, themselves, and the Supreme Being, the Lord of Ultimate Love from whom all souls have originated. In this view, matter is the unconscious realm of the Supreme Reality and represents only one part of the total reality. The other part is our true transcendental home because it is conscious in nature, like us.

THE LAST STEP IS FINAL LIBERATION ✤

After experimenting for an undetermined period of time and experiencing matter in both its joys and limitations, the soul becomes ready to exit the park and return to the transcendental abode. This process of return is the graduation ceremony for those souls who have finished their learning program within matter. At that stage, the souls engage in a process of gradual disassociation from matter. They begin to divest themselves of all material self-identification. Once this is accomplished, they finally achieve a state called *moksha*, or final liberation from identification with matter. The process of becoming ready to leave the park and resume one's true eternal nature is sometimes called *yoga*. The yoga that begins with physical postures and breathing is only one of many different yogic methodologies whose purpose is to assist the souls in achieving moksha, or final liberation from the bondage to matter. The word *yoga* literally means "to link or reestablish our forgotten connection to the Source of our existence in the transcendental realm."

The real aim of yoga is not health or physical fitness, or even mental balance and peace of mind. Those are by-products of achieving a state of permanent reconnection with our true eternal nature, the Supreme Reality and Being who is the source of all, and the nonmaterial home from which we originally began our journey into the realm of matter and karma. You may remember that the material energy is called the *gu* in Sanskrit. This gu (or goo) is the source of another well-known Sanskrit term, *guru*. *Gu* means "matter" and *ru* means "who removes it." Thus the real meaning of guru is anyone who has information on how to remove the souls' material conception of life and lead them back to their original spiritual nature.

You may remember that the subtle body is the place where the seeds of previous karmas and the desires of present actions are growing. That growth can be arrested, the desires changed, and the growth of karmas prevented. Aside from the yoga of bodily postures, there are various techniques and practices that one learns from a guru that specifically remove karmas and inappropriate desires from the subtle body. By perfecting those processes it is possible for us to cultivate a divine connection that reempowers our atma (soul) to go beyond the influence of karmas. Our oldest causes and effects, or prarabda karmas (the ripe fruit of our past actions), are not altered by these yogas. Our gene codes and bodies remain the same, but our present consciousness and future karmas can be completely transformed and removed.

BY DIVINE GRACE WE CAN BURN OFF OUR KARMA ✣

If the laws of matter that cause actions to generate reactions are called the *ritam*, and if the violation of those laws of nature causes death or mritam, then the remedy for the negative effects of karma is called *amritam*. Sometimes *amrita* is called "the nectar of immortality that liberates us from death." Interestingly, our English word *nectar* is made up of two words— "nec," which means death, and "Tara," which means "she who carries us beyond." The idea here is that by some divine grace or divinely inspired process, we are able to go beyond the entire system of karma, to burn off our past karma and to live in such a way that we no longer create future karma from our present actions.

Such people are then in a state of kriyamana karma, or action that does not produce a material reaction in the future. They are becoming *jivan-mukta* and accumulate something called *sukriti*. Sukriti is spiritual merit that is collected from life to life by humans as the result of their various spiritual experiences and activities. It is not lost from birth to birth but rather grows until the atma is ready to leave matter and return to the transcendental realm. This atma is now an "old soul."

LIBERATION MEANS NOT HAVING TO RETURN ✲

E ven though such atmas are still apparently in a body within the material world, they no longer generate future reactions from their actions. They appear to be acting within the material realm, but due to their connection with the transcendental realm and the Supreme Being, they are no longer generating karmas that will bind them to future reactions. They have achieved moksha, or liberation from matter and the bondage to its laws.

One could walk by such a liberated person on the street and not notice the subtle differences in his or her consciousness, although there are subtle symptoms. According to the Vedas, those who have transcended material consciousness to a sufficient degree will not experience future reactions to the laws of cause and effect. At death they will not be taken by the agents of Yamaraja but will instead be transported to the transcendental abode. They are liberated and are in the process of graduating from the "universe-ity." They will not be returning to the material park in their next life, either as a creature, a human, or a deva.

If they do return, it will be as a guru or teacher whose mission is to help other souls find liberation. Their atmas are ready to return to the transcendental abode from which we all originated. According to the Vedas and yoga philosophy, this is the end-game of karma—to have no more karma, no more material desires, to owe nothing and be owed nothing, to have no material attachments and to be completely absorbed in awareness of the transcendental world and ready to return there, to be in this world but not of it, to be a soul who had not only a human experience but all the experiences the material world has to offer. Been there, done that, got the merit badge, ready to leave, liberated from all the rules and limitations of birth, death, old age, and disease—moksha!

This raises the question what exactly life in the transcendental realm would be like. We have been within matter for a long time before we reach the point of liberation from its grasp. Therefore, not only do we need to find the way out of the material world by removing all the unconscious goo that has covered our atmas, but we also need to learn how to behave or live in the long-forgotten transcendental realm.

The library of Vedic knowledge gives extensive information about the nature of the transcendental abode. Although we don't have space to discuss the transcendental in detail in this book dedicated to karma, a few details will help illuminate the topic. The most important thing to remember is that even in how we return to the transcendental world, we remain individuals and can exercise choice. Like crossing any border, there are certain requirements for entry. When leaving the realm of prakriti, one cannot take matter or material ideas into the transcendental. No goo is allowed there. Such things are inert in nature and can only stay within the material realm.

The final knowledge of the Veda is called *Vedanta*, the knowledge of the ultimate end toward which all souls are headed when they return to the transcendental. The Vedanta literature describes that the transcendental region has a variety of places for all the souls to choose from. Just as in matter, there are many galaxies and planets, so in the transcendental realm there are many abodes where life is experienced in a wide variety of ways. Some souls return to the transcendental with the desire to merge their own small being into the Supreme Being. It is as if a small light joined a big light to shine together. These souls would go to live in the "impersonal" area of the transcendental called the impersonal Brahman.

The other choice is based on the idea that the Supreme Reality is also a Supreme Person with whom all souls have the ability to enter into a loving relationship. In this second form of liberation into the transcendental, learning to love in a very pure way is the prerequisite to entering into the more personal areas of the transcendental abode. There, the many eternal beings headed by the Supreme Transcendental Being engage in a wide variety of creative and enjoyable activities uninterrupted by the problems we experienced within matter. That Supreme Person or God is called Bhagavan.

In the transcendental realm though, there is no power-based relationship between the souls and Bhagavan (God). The relationships are all sweet and loving. Such love is hard for us to comprehend while we are within the material world since here we see pain and suffering everywhere, but the Vedas say that such sweet loving worlds exist inside the Brahman where Bhagavan and his friends and lovers remain for eternity. Since we have forgotten the transcendental realm, part of returning is not only removing the goo but reactivating our loving nature to its fullest extent by a yoga that restores our lost love for Bhagavan. That learning is necessary in order to return to the personal realms of the transcendental.

It is our choice to return to the transcendental realm and to return to either the personal or impersonal areas. Yet in order to go to either, we must become qualified through the practice of a yogic process that helps restore our true eternal nature and become truly liberated souls. The Vedas are filled with stories and accounts of such liberated souls. We see this impulse for getting free from the limitations of the material world in many traditions. The Vedas would say this is because it is our true nature to desire eternal freedom, love, joy, beauty, and complete consciousness. On the one hand, the laws of karma are the necessary rules of living within the temporary material realm. Yet everyone knows within their hearts that they long for unlimited life without restriction. The Vedas say such a life is possible. It exists in the realms beyond our current perception. Whether this is true or not cannot be "proven," but the great souls of all cultures and times do say it can be experienced within the core of our true being. In the final analysis, only your own experience will give you the answer.

CHAPTER 8

QUESTIONS AND ANSWERS ON KARMA

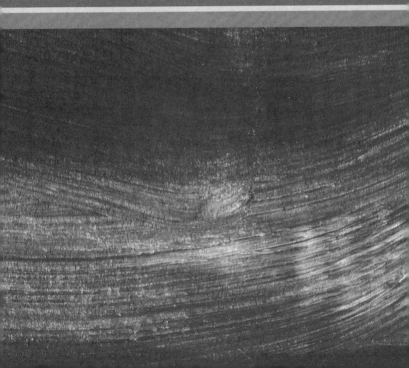

Questions and Answers

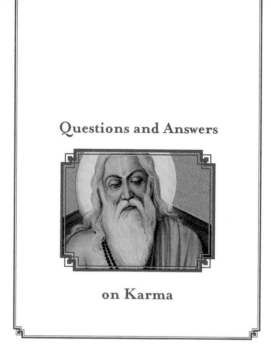

on Karma

Animals evolve, humans involve.

This chapter is designed to answer some of the most common questions asked regarding the theory of karma.

Q. If we have had many births in the past, why do we forget them?

A. The material energy, or *prakriti*, is called the unconscious energy not only because it is unconscious, but because by associating with it, we become unconscious. We are born unconscious, wrapped in the coverings of matter, and in the course of our lives we forget many things. We learn things and then forget them.

We have dreams and visions and then forget them. Therefore, forgetfulness is not a proof of the nonexistence of something. This unconscious aspect of matter is so formidable that yogis say that there is really only one enemy in this world— ignorance and forgetfulness of our true nature.

Q. There are billions more people on our planet than just a few hundred years ago. If reincarnation is a true theory, where do all the new souls come from?

A. Think of all the many species of life as a grand pyramid with human beings at the apex of the triangle. There are always large numbers of souls moving upward from below us in the many species. They are constantly moving toward human life. The problem in the material world is not a shortage of souls but rather a shortage of graduates.

Q. What happens to the soul who tries to achieve liberation but somehow does not succeed?

A. According to the Vedas, if someone pursues liberation with determination but somehow does not attain that goal in one lifetime, he takes his next birth on the higher planets of the devas. To make an earthly comparison, imagine a hard-working person winning a one-year vacation to Hawaii. After his or her deva vacation, the soul is placed in a good family for his or her next birth, with opportunities to continue his or her journey on the path of liberation.

Q. It looks like karma is an endless process. If that is so, what is the purpose of human life here on Earth?

A. According to the Vedas, the purpose of life on Earth is the evolution of souls in the direction of liberation. In this view, there is no particular end goal of history or final plan for being on Earth. It is just like attending a school. The purpose of the school is the education and evolution of the individual students. Other than that, the school has no separate purpose. For this reason, the karmic view is that we should maintain the Earth in perfect condition for future generations of students.

In recent times, this idea has come to be known as ecology. Previously, it was considered to be a sacred responsibility for each generation to leave the school in good shape for the next generation. Obviously, not everyone holds this view of our reason for being here. India has been trying to preserve this ideal for thousands of years, though in the last few thousand years, the forces of chaos have caused much damage to the peaceful idea of Earth as a school.

Q. Do we receive karma for killing the food we eat and is there much difference in the karma from our various choices?

A. Think again of the pyramid of spiritual evolution. We humans are the only species that does not have its food choices controlled by instinct. Thus, food choices are some of the most critical and potentially damaging we can make both for ourselves and the planet. According to the yogic theory, the higher we eat on the food chain, the more disturbance is caused in our environment. This is the main reason for adopting a vegetarian or mostly vegetarian diet. For example, to raise one bull for slaughter as food for humans requires thousands of gallons of water, creates large amounts of waste, needs acres of grazing land, and produces only a relatively small amount of food protein. It is a terribly inefficient means of producing food for humans, not to speak of the violence to the animal and toxins produced by its slaughter. If the same resources were used for producing vegetarian food, thousands more people could be fed.

The modern statistics in this regard are that if we converted from beef as food to vegetarian foods, we could feed a billion more people with the same resources. Therefore, what we choose to eat as humans is much more than a personal preference or matter of taste. Our eating creates a series of causes and effects that support or displace life on Earth in complex ways for which we the consumers are held accountable. Consumers are not free from reaction simply by closing their eyes to the process. Violating these and other similar laws of nature have future consequences for the soul on many levels of responsibility.

Q. If being in this material world is so problematic, why did the souls choose to come here in the first place and why did the Supreme Being allow them to make such a dangerous choice?

A. One might also ask the question: "At what point would you like your freedom of choice taken away?" In fact there are many subtle differences in the answers to this question. Many schools of thought have accepted parts of karma theory, such as cause and effect or reincarnation, but not all are in agreement on this particular topic of individuality and free will. The widely accepted Vedic view is that we are divine in nature, which includes the right to explore all the different areas of the total existence of the Supreme Being.

Both the transcendental realm and this material realm
are divine. But since we are distinctive individual sparks
of divinity, we are eternally invested with free will. Using
that ability to choose, we can request to explore either the
conscious or unconscious realms of existence. With this
in mind, in order to be here, we had to be the ones who
exercised that choice in order to continue our exploration of
both our own nature and limitations as well as those of the
Supreme Being.

The Vedas say that although we are conscious by nature, we
can get lost in the realm of the unconscious because it is so
much larger than our power of consciousness can illuminate.
In our own bodies we experience this. I am directly conscious
of my body, the matter in it is pervaded by my consciousness,
but I am unable to pervade the bodies of others or the world
around me. In this sense, the definition of God or the
Supreme Being would be: "that consciousness that pervades
all of matter as well as the entire transcendental realm." The
difference between us and the Supreme Consciousness is that
we can get lost during our explorations of the unconscious
realms of matter. For this reason, the Supreme Being is
eternally sending search parties to the world of matter to assist
us in finding the way back home.

Q. Can large groups of souls have a karmic relationship
with each other?

A. Nations, cities, religions, races, tribes, villages, families,
gangs, corporations, and all such groupings have a conscious
idea about why they are together. That idea is often the action
of their rational minds making sense out of a connection
from the surface. If the same groupings are viewed from the
devas' perspective, they are arranged to facilitate the acting out

of various karmic agendas that may have been carried forward for many lifetimes. We see only the surface facts and try to extrapolate the plot from a few details.

The devas see the big picture, the part we have forgotten. Thus karma theory explains how we are truly players in dramas we seldom fully understand. Once understood, this view helps to remove the many artificial barriers that divide us. We have all taken birth in every gender, sect, race, party, or viewpoint imaginable. As such, this view engenders humility, understanding, compassion, and a sense that we are all part of one divine family. We are all students in the same school in spite of our differences in curriculum or view at any time. The ideal of karmic philosophy is that we will become less competitive and more cooperative as we work toward our ultimate and relative goals.

Ahamkara: Indicates a subtle energy of matter which, when combined with the consciousness of the atma, creates the idea that we come from and are matter. Also known as the false ego.

Akasha (Akashic): The fifth of the dense material elements (earth, water, fire, air, space). Akasha is often translated as space or the accommodating principle that is filled with subtle vibrations or cosmic rays.

Amrita: A mysterious liquid substance that was the final product of the churning of the milk ocean by the demigods (devas) and demons (asuras). Amrita, or the nectar of immortality, was then fed to the devas so they could perform their various jobs of maintaining the universe. Amrita also refers to anything that counteracts the influence of death or disease due to violating the laws of material nature.

Atma: The true self that cannot die.

Ayurveda: Ayus means life; Ayurveda is the medical system based on Vedic wisdom. It creates well-being by supporting the life force in various ways.

Bhagavan: The Supreme Person who is the possessor of all opulence.

Chitragupta: The deva who acts as the court reporter in Yamaraja's court of death and judgment.

Deva (Devi, feminine): Derived from the Sanskrit "div," meaning to play in the light. Also called the divine helpers, they are souls just like humans or animals, but they have attained posts in the administration of the laws of material nature. They work for Vishnu and Lakshmi in the function of maintaining nature.

Dharma: Based on the root "dhri," which means the essential nature of a thing, which if it is taken away, the thing is no longer itself. The dharma of fire is to burn, the dharma of water is to be liquid. The dharma of a person arises from the essential nature of his or her body. From that come certain powers and from those certain duties in the use of those powers. This is called svadharma, or a person's own dharma. Finally, the soul's eternal nature is called its Sanatana Dharma, or its immortal nature.

Jiva: Another term indicating the atma or eternal soul. Jiva also means life or the soul in contact with the life force within matter, thus jiva-atma.

Jyotisha: The Sanskrit name for astrology. It means the science of how life is regulated by light.

Karma: Derived from the Sanskrit "kri," which means to do. The law of cause and effect.

Kriyamana: Actions on behalf of the Supreme Being that do not generate karmic reactions.

Manas (Manusha): This word is derived from the Sanskrit for mind. Applied to humans, it means possessing free will or having a mind of one's own.

Maya: Literally "not this," referring to the state of consciousness in which the atma assumes that the material reality is permanent and not causally dependent upon the Supreme Being.

Moksha: Also sometimes known as mukti. This word describes the state of a soul who has become liberated from all material entanglement and is focused upon the transcendental.

Mritam: Death, as the final outcome of violating the ritam or laws of nature.

Prakriti: That which is controlled by a greater Being; matter is called *apara-prakriti*, or the unconscious energy of the Supreme. The transcendental realm is called *para-prakriti* or the conscious realm of Divine energy.

Prarabda: This is the cause and effect that is currently manifesting as our destinies or the ripe fruit of our past actions.

Ritam: The invisible laws embedded in material nature. These rules govern all action and reaction within matter.

Samsara: Reincarnation or the repeated cycle of birth and death experienced by the eternal souls once they enter the realm of matter. Sometimes described as the wheel of birth and death.

Sanatana: Eternal or everlasting. When this word occurs along with dharma as "Sanatana Dharma," it means the true eternal nature of the atma.

Sanchitta: Used to describe the potential or future karmas that are figuratively described as seeds in the mind or subtle body. If they are not removed, they will produce fruit in the future.

Sanskrit: The name of the language in which the Vedas of India were written. The word literally means perfected, implying that Sanskrit is very scientific and consistent.

Sukriti: The merit accumulated from various forms of spiritual activity. This accumulates over lifetimes and is not used up or temporary like material karma.

Tantra: Literally means that which expands or to weave, and is the source of the English word tension. Everything in the material world is held together by a certain correct tension. Sexuality is one small subject within tantra, which is similar to the word science but is more holistic.

Tara: A devi who is known for healing and protection. Her name means to deliver or carry across. The idea is that she saves one from karmic troubles.

Vedas: A large collection of sacred writings originating in ancient India. They are considered to be one of the integral scriptural foundations of Hinduism. Many Hindus believe that the Vedas were not written by anyone, including Ishvara (the term used for God), but are eternally existing.

Vedic: Vedic may refer to ancient India, the Vedic period, the Vedas or the historical Vedic religion.

Vrata: Vow or promise. Since humans have free will, they do not act only from instinct like animals or under the ritam like devas. Instead, they act through giving their word as a promise.

Yamaraja: The superintendent of death and karmic justice.

Yoga: To link or connect. Our English word yoke is derived from yoga. This idea is that through certain specific actions, one is able to reestablish his or her lost link to the Supreme Being in the transcendental realm.

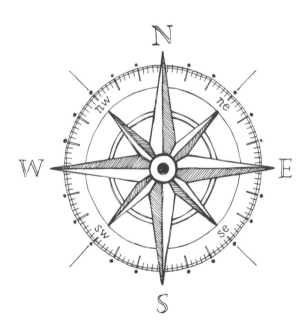

ACKNOWLEDGMENTS ✼

My gratitude and appreciation goes first to my wife and partner Sandi Graham for all she has done to make this book possible. My many thanks go to Richelle Jarrell who typed, proofread, and edited the manuscript. My appreciation also goes to the creative staff at Mandala Publishing, who are dedicated to publishing beautiful books on important topics of spiritual value to the world. Finally, I would like to thank my editor Arjuna VD Kooij for his suggestions and contributions that helped greatly in perfecting this book.

ABOUT THE AUTHOR ✼

JEFFREY ARMSTRONG (Kavindra Rishi)
A Western Master of Eastern Wisdom
Inspirational Speaker, Visionary Spiritual Teacher, Author & Founder of VASA (Vedic Academy of Arts and Sciences)

Initiated by Masters of the mystical Eastern Traditions, Jeffrey Armstrong is a charismatic speaker and counselor who teaches the Philosophy of Yoga as a way of being, and Enlightenment as a way of life. As a student and scholar of the Vedic Philosophy for over forty-five years, Jeffrey has mastered Raja Yoga, Tantra, and Mantra practices. Jeffrey uses humor, passion, and spiritual insights to address the needs of our current relationships. Jeffrey is also an award-winning author and mystical poet, with degrees in psychology, literature, and history & comparative religion.

www.JeffreyArmstrong.com

NOTES

NOTES

NOTES

NOTES

NOTES

MANDALA

An Imprint of MandalaEarth
PO Box 3088
San Rafael, CA 94912
www.MandalaEarth.com

Find us on Facebook: www.facebook.com/MandalaEarth
Follow us on Twitter: @MandalaEarth

Library of Congress Cataloging-in-Publication Data available.

ISBN: 978-1-68383-380-2

Publisher: Raoul Goff
Associate Publisher: Phillip Jones
Senior Editor: Rossella Barry
Editorial Assistant: Tessa Murphy
Senior Production Editor: Rachel Anderson
Production Manager: Sam Taylor
Designer: Amy DeGrote

The content of this book is provided for informational purposes only
and is not intended to diagnose, treat, or cure any conditions without
the assistance of a trained practitioner. If you are experiencing any
medical condition, seek care from an appropriate licensed professional.

ROOTS of PEACE   REPLANTED PAPER

Mandala Publishing, in association with Roots of Peace, will plant
two trees for each tree used in the manufacturing of this book. Roots
of Peace is an internationally renowned humanitarian organization
dedicated to eradicating land mines worldwide and converting war-
torn lands into productive farms and wildlife habitats. Roots of Peace
will plant two million fruit and nut trees in Afghanistan and provide
farmers there with the skills and support necessary for sustainable
land use.

Manufactured in China by Insight Editions

10 9 8 7 6 5 4 3 2 1